When We Became FOUR

A MEMORY BOOK for THE WHOLE FAMILY

JILL CARYL WEINER

Author of *When We Became Three*

PLAIN SIGHT PUBLISHING
AN IMPRINT OF CEDAR FORT, INC.
SPRINGVILLE, UT

Lyrics from "Wedding Song," written by Bob Dylan, Copyright © 1973 by Ram's Horn Music; renewed 2001 by Ram's Horn Music. All rights reserved. International copyright secured. Reprinted by permission.

ISBN 13: 978-1-4621-2189-2

Published by Plain Sight Publishing, an imprint of Cedar Fort, Inc.
2373 W. 700 S., Springville, UT 84663
Distributed by Cedar Fort, Inc., www.cedarfort.com

Cover and page design by Shawnda T. Craig and Katie Payne
Cover design © 2018 Cedar Fort, Inc.
Edited by Erica Myers, Deborah Spencer, and Kaitlin Barwick
Author photo by Jonas Gustavsson

Printed in Canada

10 9 8 7 6 5 4 3 2 1

Contents

Congratulations!

You are an awesome family embarking on your next great adventure: your second baby. As Baby is adjusting to the world and transforming into the cutest little person, your precious first child is learning to share the spotlight with an adorable demanding costar and adjusting to the sometimes bumpy, sometimes blissful, often baffling job of becoming a Big Sib. As parents, you are juggling it all. The adventure you're beginning belongs to Four.

When We Became Four is a low-maintenance, pressure-free, wise-yet-whimsical way to capture all the milestones and special moments of your growing family. Many of these pages can be filled out as a family to celebrate each stage in Baby's life and the richness of your changing family dynamic. It's a great way to promote good will between Baby and Big Sib and document their remarkable budding relationship. Since this book is based on memories and feelings you can fill it out as Baby grows or even years down the line. Make it your own! Check multiple boxes, add dates, drawings, photos, or thoughts. The result is a keepsake journal that will have the whole family laughing, reflecting, and reminiscing for years to come.

As a family, your lives and memories are forever intertwined. Let the pages of this book tell your story.

—Jill

When We Became Two

When We Became Two

Our story begins before we were even a family. It starts with the **(circle as many that fit or add your own)** magical, miserable, mundane, _____ moment in time when Mommy and Daddy first met. It's a _____ story. We met when/because _____.

It was a(n) _____ first meeting. This is the short version of what happened: _____

_____.

Since we became Two, a lot of _____ things have happened. One **(circle one or more)** funny, interesting, memorable thing that happened was _____

_____

_____.

We loved being together because _____

_____. We

both enjoyed _____

and _____ and our favorite times

together were when _____. Another great

memory we have together is _____

_____.

Here's the story of how we met and what things were like before you and Big Sib came along.

It's when we opened the door to becoming Four.

> "You can't blame gravity for falling in love."
>
> ALBERT EINSTEIN

WHEN WE MET, IT WAS LIKE

- [ ] Fireworks—we felt sparks flying
- [ ] Castanets—we really clicked
- [ ] A soft drizzling rain—safe and comfortable
- [ ] An earthquake—what a disaster
- [ ] A Tuesday morning—nothing out of the ordinary
- [ ] Other: _____

Here's the quick version of the story: _____

_____

_____

_____

_____

_____

_____

_____

_____

_____

IN THOSE EARLY DAYS

- [ ] We knew we'd be together forever.
- [ ] We started as friends and love grew from friendship.
- [ ] We couldn't stand each other.
- [ ] One of us took an interest before the other.
- [ ] Other: _____

> "I love you more than ever and I haven't yet begun."
>
> BOB DYLAN

IF OUR RELATIONSHIP HAD A SEASON IT WOULD BE

☐ Winter ☐ Spring ☐ Summer ☐ Fall

Because: _____

_____

_____

_____

The moment Mom knew she was in love: _____

_____

_____

_____

_____

_____

_____

The moment Dad knew he was in love: _____

_____

_____

_____

_____

_____

_____

4

"I love being married. It's so great to find that one special person you want to annoy for the rest of your life."

RITA RUDNER

The 411 on Us

Our song: _____

Our favorite restaurant(s): _____

Our typical date: _____
_____
_____

A perfect evening we've had: _____
_____
_____

A favorite outing we've had: _____
_____
_____

Other things we like to do together: _____
_____
_____
_____
_____

> "I love you not only for what you are,
> but for what I am when I am with you."
>
> ELIZABETH BARRETT BROWNING

Most romantic moment(s): _____

_____

_____

_____

Funniest moment(s) in courtship or relationship: _____

_____

_____

_____

Scariest moment(s) in courtship or relationship: _____

_____

_____

_____

🕐 TIME CAPSULE

If we were making a time capsule about our relationship
before we became parents, we would be sure to include:

_____

_____

_____

_____

When We Were Three

When We Became Three

When Big Sib came along on _____, our spontaneous romantic **(circle all that apply or add your own)** days, dinners, walks, conversations, movies, vacations _____ got swept up in caring for a little tornado of love. It was **(circle all that apply or add your own)** amazing, challenging, life-altering, _____. Some of the biggest changes or challenges were_____. We had to learn how to _____ and _____. But it was also a lot of fun! We really loved _____together.

It was so exciting when Big Sib started to _____.

Big Sib's favorite things to do were _____

and _____.

Our favorite times together as a family were when we _____

_____

_____

_____.

Could we ask for anything more? What if we became Four!

ADD A PHOTO OF WHEN
WE BECAME THREE

The Pre-You Us

Things Mom and Dad love about Big Sib: _____

_____

_____

_____

_____

Things Big Sib loves about Mom and Dad: _____

_____

_____

_____

_____

Other special people in our lives: _____

_____

_____

_____

_____

Family Moments

Funny moments: _____
_____
_____

Scary moments: _____
_____
_____

Precious moments: _____
_____
_____

Any good stories? _____
_____
_____
_____
_____

Movies we love that we can't wait to share with you:
_____
_____

Books we love that we can't wait to share with you:
_____
_____
_____

Use this space for anything!

(Memories, details, thoughts, photos, drawings or even stickers.)

Work, School & Day to Day

We love spending the day together,
but it's not always possible.

 **MOM**

I usually spend my days _____

On weekends I like to _____

My dream job would be _____

Something you might not know about me is _____

_____

_____

DAD

I usually spend my days _____

On weekends I like to _____

My dream job would be _____

Something you might not know about me is _____

_____

_____

BIG SIB

I usually spend my days _____
_____
_____

On weekends I like to _____
_____
_____

Some of my favorite things to do are _____
_____
_____

Something you might not know about me is _____
_____
_____

My parents imagine my dream job might be _____
_____
_____

- Us -

Some of our favorite things to do together are _____
_____
_____

Great Expectations!

WE WANTED TO HAVE YOU

- ☐ Right away
- ☐ After a little while so we'd be ready
- ☐ Other: _____

MOM

WHAT SIGNS POINTED YOU TO TAKING A PREGNANCY TEST?

- ☐ My cycle quit cycling.
- ☐ I developed a superhero's sense of smell.
- ☐ Anything I put down came back up.
- ☐ I was too exhausted to reach for the remote.
- ☐ I felt a little too fabulous.
- ☐ I felt the same way when I was pregnant with Big Sib.
- ☐ Other: _____

HOW YOU FELT WHEN IT CAME BACK POSITIVE:

- ☐ Elated
- ☐ Freaked out!
- ☐ Complete
- ☐ Unprepared
- ☐ Energized
- ☐ Ready for the challenge
- ☐ Other: _____

How you told Dad: _____

_____

Dad's reaction: _____

_____

Big Sib Finds Out!

REACTION

- ☐ Yay! I'm going to be a Big Sib!
- ☐ Where will we put it?
- ☐ What about me?
- ☐ Will I get to name it?
- ☐ Gaga (Too young to understand.)
- ☐ Other: _____

EXPLANATION ABOUT WHERE BABY
WILL COME FROM:

- ☐ Stork
- ☐ Birds and Bees
- ☐ Babies-Я-Us
- ☐ Amazon

When and where we told our family: _____

_____

_____

How we told our friends: _____

_____

_____

Favorite reactions: _____

_____

_____

_____

You're on the Way!

EVERYONE IS SO HAPPY FOR US BECAUSE WE'RE EXPECTING YOU, A NEW BABY. BUT FOR US, YOU'RE SO MUCH MORE.

MOM SEES YOU AS

☐ Another child to care for and love
☐ A companion and lifelong friend for Big Sib
☐ A future playmate and shopping buddy
☐ Someone to coach or guide
☐ Other: _____

DAD SEES YOU AS

☐ Another child to care for and love
☐ A companion and lifelong friend for Big Sib
☐ A playmate for himself
☐ Someone to coach or guide
☐ Other: _____

BIG SIB SEES YOU AS

☐ A brother or sister
☐ A best friend and playmate
☐ A present or toy
☐ A student to teach and care for
☐ Someone to babysit
☐ Goo Goo, Gah Gah—has no idea what's coming.
☐ Other: _____

Details and thoughts: _____

_____

_____

_____

_____

"To describe my mother would be to write about a hurricane in its perfect power. Or the climbing, falling colors of a rainbow."

MAYA ANGELOU

They Bring Out the Best

Personality traits, qualities, and/or physical attributes we want Baby to inherit from Dad: _____

_____

_____

Personality traits, qualities, and/or physical attributes we want Baby to inherit from Mom: _____

_____

_____

Big Sib's personality traits, qualities, and/or physical attributes we want Baby to share: _____

_____

_____

_____

_____

_____

_____

_____

Pickle-Flavored Potato Chips and Triple-Fudge Ice Cream

 **MOM**

Food Cravings: _____

Repulsions: _____

Any senses on overdrive? _____

WHICH OF THE SEVEN PREGNANT DWARFS WERE YOU?

- ☐ Happy
- ☐ Sleepy
- ☐ Moody
- ☐ Busy
- ☐ Nervous
- ☐ Queasy
- ☐ Other: _____

(Enormous? Loving? Weepy?)

 **DAD**

WHICH OF THE SEVEN EXPECTANT DADS WERE YOU?

- ☐ Happy
- ☐ Sleepy
- ☐ Nervous
- ☐ Loving
- ☐ Busy
- ☐ Helpful
- ☐ Other: _____

(Sweet? Argumentative? Agreeable?)

Most challenging pregnancy-related
request(s) from Mom: _____

_____

"So where did these cravings come from?
I concluded it's the baby ordering in."

PAUL REISER

 **BIG SIB**

WHICH OF THE SEVEN ADORABLE
FUTURE SIBLINGS WERE YOU?

- ☐ Joyous
- ☐ Jealous
- ☐ Cuddly
- ☐ Clingy
- ☐ Clueless
- ☐ Playful
- ☐ Nervous
- ☐ Other: _____

(Silly? Serious? Super-Cute?)

Details, thoughts, drawing, or a photo:

Every Silver Lining
Has at Least a Small Cloud

Best thing about being pregnant: _____
_____
_____

Worst thing about being pregnant: _____
_____
_____

Mom's Biggest Concerns about Becoming Four: _____
_____
_____
_____

Dad's Biggest Concerns about Becoming Four: _____
_____
_____
_____

Big Sib's Biggest Concerns about Becoming Four:
_____
_____
_____

Help!!

WHERE DO WE PUT THE BABY?

- ☐ It's easy—we have plenty of room.
- ☐ Sharing is caring.
- ☐ Finally we get to redecorate!
- ☐ There goes the den!
- ☐ OMG!
- ☐ Time to house hunt!
- ☐ Other: _____

Details and thoughts: _____

_____

_____

_____

_____

_____

_____

BABY INVASION PREPAREDNESS CHECKLIST

- ☐ Decorate or rearrange
- ☐ Get baby stuff out of storage
- ☐ Buy bassinet, crib, etc., to replace baby things given away
- ☐ Pack a bag for the hospital
- ☐ Sign Big Sib up for a what-to-expect class about being a Big Sib
- ☐ Create a plan for Big Sib for the big day and reach out to all involved
- ☐ Other: _____

> "Everybody wants to save the Earth;
> nobody wants to help Mom do the dishes."

P.J. O'ROURKE

Plan Ahead!

The Match Made in Heaven Game

Rules: (1) Make sure Mom and Dad are both in an agreeable mood; **(2)** match yourselves with your future baby-related responsibilities. Sharing is encouraged!

Mom	Dad	
☐	☐	Sending the baby announcements
☐	☐	Changing diapers
☐	☐	Acting as baby fashion police
☐	☐	Preparing & cooking food or ordering in
☐	☐	Getting up at night with Baby
☐	☐	Doing laundry
☐	☐	Keeping up the family blog
☐	☐	Doing the dishes
☐	☐	Bathing Baby
☐	☐	Baby photographer
☐	☐	Taking Big Sib out so Mom can nap
☐	☐	Other: _____

Helpful advice from others: _____

_____

_____

Weird advice from others: _____

_____

_____

> "The price of greatness is responsibility."
>
> WINSTON CHURCHILL

The Match Made in Heaven Game

Big Sib Version

Check off the many ways even a little Big Sib can help.

Rules: (1) Make sure Big Sib is in an agreeable mood; **(2)** match Big Sib with future baby-related responsibilities. As with this whole book, if Big Sib is too young to talk, use your imagination.

Big Sib

- [ ] Making Baby laugh
- [ ] Singing to Baby
- [ ] Helping dress Baby
- [ ] Reading to Baby
- [ ] Playing with Baby (i.e., peekaboo)
- [ ] Changing diapers (or helping)
- [ ] Baby's stylist
- [ ] Babysitting
- [ ] Keeping Baby busy so Mom can nap
- [ ] Other: _____

Songs Big Sib is going to sing to Baby: _____

_____

_____

_____

_____

_____

> "Those are my principles.
> If you don't like them, I have others."

GROUCHO MARX

Parenting principles we agree on: _____
_____
_____

Parenting principles we're still trying to
convince each other to adopt: _____
_____
_____

Things we will do differently: _____
_____
_____

Things we will do the same: _____
_____
_____
_____

ARGUMENTS WE'VE HAD:

- ☐ What to name Baby
- ☐ What to tell Big Sib about how babies are made
- ☐ Whether to find out Baby's gender beforehand
- ☐ Whether to tell Baby's gender or name to others
- ☐ Whether Dad has to switch to decaf coffee too
- ☐ Other: _____

WAITING FOR YOU IS LIKE WAITING

- ☐ For cake to rise—we know you will be sweet and delicious
- ☐ For a train—we want you to take us to our next destination
- ☐ For a roller coaster—we can't wait for the thrill ride
- ☐ For a hurricane—we're not sure we're prepared
- ☐ For rain in a drought—we really want you to come already!
- ☐ Other: _____

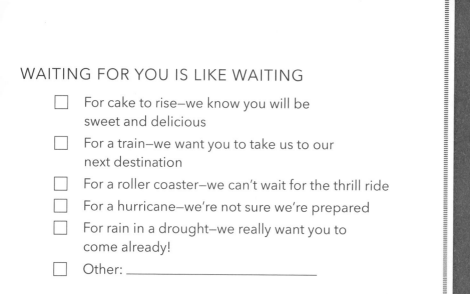 TIME CAPSULE

If we were making a time capsule about our family before Baby came along, we would be sure to include:

_____

_____

_____

"As Daddy said, life is 95 percent anticipation."

GLORIA SWANSON

Memories we can't wait to make with Baby: _____

_____

_____

_____

_____

> "Everything grows rounder and wider and weirder, and I sit here in the middle of it all and wonder who in the world you will turn out to be."

CARRIE FISHER

A Letter to Baby

(Write now or later from one person or the whole family.)

Date: _____

_____

_____

_____

_____

_____

_____

_____

_____

_____

ADD A FAMILY PHOTO
OR MOM'S BABY BUMP

When We Became Four

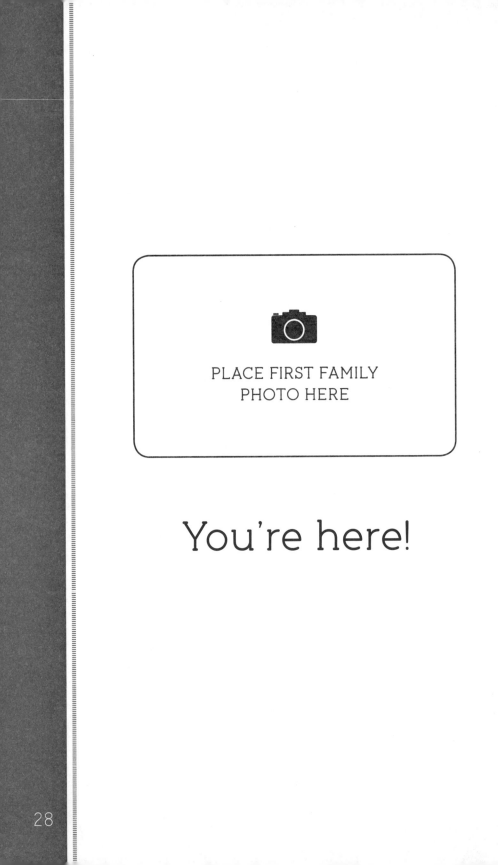

PLACE FIRST FAMILY
PHOTO HERE

You're here!

When We Became Four

You made your grand entrance to the world on _____.

We knew you were coming because _____.

Mom **(circle one)** said, screamed, felt _____ and
Dad _____.

We called _____. Big Sib _____

_____.

The original plan was _____

_____.

Here's what really happened _____

_____

_____. When you arrived, we felt so

_____ and _____.

We couldn't believe _____.

Who knew you'd be so _____!

We decided to call you _____ because

_____. These loved ones wanted

to see you right away: _____

_____

_____.

Your birth added a new dimension to our world.

We can't wait to see what's in store now that we've become Four!

> "Every child begins the world again."

HENRY DAVID THOREAU

The Labor Room:
A Judgment-Free Zone

MOM GAVE BIRTH

- ☐ At home
- ☐ In a hospital
- ☐ In the back of a car
- ☐ In a bathtub
- ☐ Other: _____

WHILE MOM WAS GIVING BIRTH, DAD WAS

- ☐ Holding Mom's hand
- ☐ Hiding under the bed
- ☐ Running the show
- ☐ Taking care of Big Sib
- ☐ Trying to find the doctor
- ☐ Other: _____

Big Sib was: _____

_____

THE DELIVERY DOCTOR/MIDWIFE WAS

- ☐ Magical
- ☐ Professional
- ☐ A linebacker
- ☐ Kind and funny
- ☐ A tough taskmaster
- ☐ Other: _____

The Do's and Don'ts of Childbirth

Aspects that were absolutely perfect: _____

_____

_____

_____

_____

Something we might have done differently: _____

_____

_____

_____

_____

Details and thoughts about this special day: _____

_____

_____

_____

_____

PLACE PHOTO OF
MOM AND BABY HERE

Introducing Us!

"You're something between a dream and a miracle."

ELIZABETH BARRETT BROWNING

It's a Baby!
(AND MORE!)

Name: _____

Date and time of birth: _____

Location: _____

Length: _____

Weight: _____

Eye color: _____

Hair color: _____

Hairstyle:

☐ Fuzz ☐ Mohawk ☐ Cue ball ☐ Other: _____

☐ You're a little sister!
☐ You're a little brother!
☐ You're a playmate!
☐ You'll be a lifelong friend!
☐ You're the cutest little squishy thing ever!
☐ You're a beloved child.
☐ You're our little _____.

> "My mother groaned, my father wept,
> into the dangerous world I leapt."
>
> WILLIAM BLAKE

WHEN YOU CAME OUT, YOU WERE

- ☐ Sleeping peacefully
- ☐ Bright red and bursting
- ☐ Twisting and shouting
- ☐ Calmly looking around
- ☐ Absolutely beautiful
- ☐ Other: _____

BABY LOOKS LIKE (CHECK ALL THAT APPLY)

- ☐ Mom
- ☐ Dad
- ☐ Big Sib
- ☐ Grandma or Grandpa
- ☐ Yoda (only cuter)
- ☐ A perfect baby doll
- ☐ Other: _____

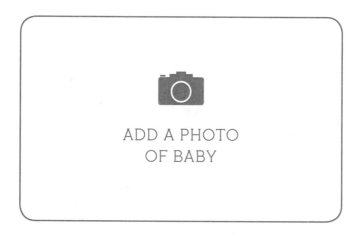

ADD A PHOTO
OF BABY

> "I am here. I brought my whole self to you.
> I am your mother."

MAYA ÀNGELOU

It's a Mom!
(AGAIN!)

Name: _____

Circle your Mom name(s):

Mom   Mama   Mommy   Best Mom Ever

Madre   Mami   The Boss   Other: _____

Birth date: _____

Height in heels or flats: _____

Hair color (at the time): _____

Interests and hobbies: _____

_____

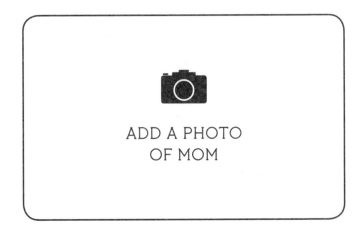

ADD A PHOTO
OF MOM

"The heart of a father is the masterpiece of nature."

ABBÉ PRÉVOST

It's a Dad!
(AGAIN!)

Name: _____

Circle your Dad name(s):

Dad   Daddy   Dada   Dude   Best Dad Ever

Poppy   Sir   Coach   Papa   Other: _____

Birth date: _____

Height in dreams (or reality): _____

Hair: ☐ Yes   ☐ No   ☐ On its way out

Interests and hobbies: _____

_____

ADD A PHOTO
OF DAD

"Brothers and sisters are as close as hands and feet."

VIETNAMESE PROVERB

It's a Big Sib!

Name: _____

Nickname: _____

Birthday: _____

Interests: _____

_____

Some details and thoughts about Big Sib: _____

_____

Best friend before Baby came along: _____

_____

What you think Baby might call you: _____

Space for a drawing or thoughts by Big Sib:

WHEN YOU SAW BABY, YOU

- ☐ Wanted to hold Baby more than anything
- ☐ Wanted to return Baby
- ☐ Didn't really care
- ☐ Cried
- ☐ Laughed
- ☐ Other: _____

WERE YOU ALLOWED TO HOLD BABY?

- ☐ Yes
- ☐ No
- ☐ GooGoo GaGa
- ☐ Yes, held a toe
- ☐ Other: _____

Details and thoughts: _____

_____

_____

_____

_____

_____

ADD A PHOTO OF
BIG SIB WITH BABY

> "A baby is something you carry inside you for nine months, in your arms for three years, and in your heart till the day you die."

MARY MASON

It's a Mom!

MY FEELINGS UPON SEEING YOU
FOR THE FIRST TIME:

- ☐ Joy
- ☐ Awe
- ☐ Fear
- ☐ Love
- ☐ Pride
- ☐ Relief
- ☐ Other: _____

THE FIRST TIME I HELD YOU, YOU WERE

- ☐ In a perfect, peaceful sleep
- ☐ Writhing like you'd jump out of my arms
- ☐ Turning colors like a chameleon
- ☐ Comfortable in my arms
- ☐ Crying inconsolably
- ☐ Other: _____

Details and thoughts: _____

_____

_____

_____

_____

_____

> "Being a dad is, you know,
> it's a surfboard on a rainbow."

It's a Dad!

MY FEELINGS UPON SEEING YOU
FOR THE FIRST TIME:

- ☐ Joy
- ☐ Awe
- ☐ Fear
- ☐ Love
- ☐ Pride
- ☐ Relief
- ☐ Other: _____

THE FIRST TIME I HELD YOU, YOU WERE

- ☐ In a perfect, peaceful sleep
- ☐ Writhing like you'd jump out of my arms
- ☐ Turning colors like a chameleon
- ☐ Comfortable in my arms
- ☐ Crying inconsolably
- ☐ Other: _____

Details and thoughts: _____

_____

_____

_____

_____

_____

"Naming a baby is an act of poetry."

RICHARD EYRE

Baby's Name

We named you _____

because _____.

Big Sib wanted to call you _____

BECAUSE OF A FAVORITE

- ☐ Stuffed animal
- ☐ Action hero or princess
- ☐ Movie star, musician, or celebrity
- ☐ Other: _____

Names we liked but couldn't agree on: _____
_____

Silliest names we considered: _____
_____

We might call you _____ as a nickname.

What we called you before you were born: _____

Notes or stories: _____
_____
_____

> "The cool part about naming your kid
> is you don't have to add six numbers
> to make sure the name is available."

BILL MURRAY

Family's Names

Mom was named _____
because _____.

Dad was named _____
because _____.

Big Sib was named _____
because _____.

Nicknames: _____
_____

Notes or stories about Baby's name or other names in
the family: _____
_____
_____

OTHER IMPORTANT NAMES:
Pediatrician: _____

Grandparents, Godparents, or Go-to friends: _____
_____
_____

> "There is not a word yet
> for old friends who have just met."
>
> JIM HENSON

Our Family, Our Village

FIRST FAMILY VISITORS

These loved ones live close and love to come see you.
Babysitting, anyone? _____

_____

_____

_____

_____

These loved ones live far away but send
you all their love: _____

_____

_____

_____

_____

We wish these loved ones were still with us: _____

_____

_____

These friends are like family: _____

_____

_____

_____

BABY FEATURE MATCH

	Mom's	Dad's	Big Sib's	Who Knows?
Eyes				
Nose				
Mouth				
Smile				
Head shape				
Ears				
Fingers				
Feet				

IF YOU WERE A BABY ANIMAL, YOU WOULD BE

- ☐ A piranha—always eating and sniping at Mom
- ☐ A koala—cuddly and always snoozing
- ☐ A puppy—joyous and mischievous
- ☐ A howler monkey—constantly wailing
- ☐ Other: _____

IF BIG SIB WAS A BABY ANIMAL, BIG SIB WOULD BE

- ☐ A penguin—cuddly and irresistible
- ☐ A bear cub—playful and mischievous
- ☐ A tiger—jealous and ready to pounce
- ☐ An owl—curious and seeking wisdom
- ☐ A hawk—overprotective and keeping others away
- ☐ Other: _____

Bringing Baby Home

WHEN WE LEFT THE HOSPITAL, WE

☐ Were thrilled beyond belief
☐ Felt exhausted and in need of care
☐ Couldn't believe we were parents of two kids!
☐ Couldn't wait to _____
☐ Felt overjoyed yet overwhelmed
☐ Other: _____

Stories or memories: _____
_____
_____
_____
_____
_____
_____

Baby's first address: _____
_____
_____

Why it will always be special: _____
_____
_____
_____
_____
_____
_____

The biggest challenge: _____
_____
_____
_____
_____
_____

The greatest triumph: _____
_____
_____
_____
_____
_____

The biggest adjustment: _____
_____
_____
_____
_____
_____

Silliest things we did as nervous parents of two:
_____
_____
_____
_____
_____

Details and thoughts: _____
_____
_____
_____
_____
_____

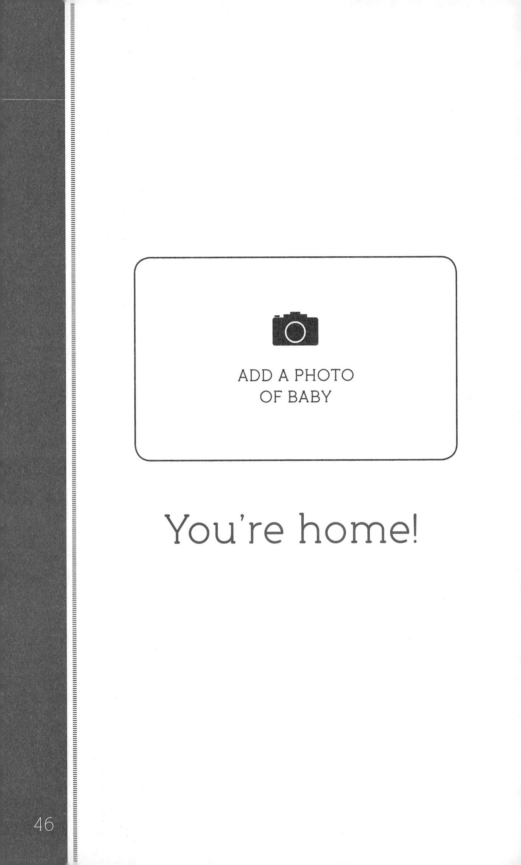

ADD A PHOTO
OF BABY

You're home!

Baby's First Months/Family's First Daze

Baby's First Months/ Family's First Daze

Those first days at home were absolutely _____. It's not every day you get a beautiful new little person to love and care for. You lit up our whole world, but we wondered what planet we were on. Your Big Sib, **(name)** _____, had been our baby for _____, and all of a sudden became the big kid of the family! It was exciting and very different. We expected _____ but were not prepared for _____.

At first, Big Sib **(circle one or add your own)** wondered, thought, said, wanted _____.

It was tricky for Big Sib to get used to _____

but soon was helping with _____. Sometimes all you seemed to want to do was **(circle as many that fit or add your own)** eat, sleep, cry, cuddle, _____, and all Big Sib wanted to do was _____ _____. Sure, taking care of a newborn and a (circle or fill-in) baby, toddler, _____-year old, teen _____ could be tricky, but it was worth every **(circle choice(s) or fill in)** wonderful, disastrous, exhausting, _____ moment.

We were tired, dazed and a bit unsure, but how wonderful it was to become Four!

All you need is love (and food,
and diaper changes, and a ton of sleep).

Baby's First Month

NOW THAT YOU'RE HOME, WE'RE SURPRISED ABOUT

- [ ] How beautiful you are
- [ ] How you arrived with your own personality
- [ ] How tricky it is to feed you
- [ ] How easy it is feed you
- [ ] How similar you are to Big Sib
- [ ] How different you are from Big Sib
- [ ] Other: _____

Details and thoughts: _____
_____
_____
_____
_____
_____
_____
_____

WE ALWAYS WANT TO REMEMBER

- [ ] How new everything feels
- [ ] How familiar this feels
- [ ] That you once fit in the crook of our arms
- [ ] How cute you and Big Sib are together
- [ ] That these days are exhausting but incredible at the same time
- [ ] Other: _____

Overjoyed! .... Overwhelmed?

Family's First Daze

WHILE YOU WERE LEARNING ABOUT THE WORLD,
WE WERE LEARNING TO CARE FOR ALL YOUR NEEDS
WHILE JUGGLING THEM WITH OURS.

When you first came home, we felt _____

BIG SIB

☐ Couldn't get enough of you
☐ Ignored you

Wanted to

☐ Return you
☐ Stuff you under the couch
☐ Put you in the washing machine
☐ Squeeze you so tight you'd either pop or poop
☐ Hold you and love you and never let you go!

☐ Other: _____

WE ADORE YOUR

☐ Puffy cheeks
☐ Beautiful eyes
☐ Abundant thighs
☐ Perfectly curled eyelashes
☐ Petal soft skin
☐ Not to mention: _____

Besides your unbelievable cuteness, we love the way you:

_____

We started calling you: _____

_____

We Knew a Lot More Than We Might Have Known, But We Didn't Know What We Didn't Know.

Some happy surprises or things we didn't expect:

_____

_____

_____

_____

_____

_____

_____

_____

YOU'RE PRACTICALLY PERFECT IN EVERY WAY. IF ONLY YOU WOULD

☐ Eat more
☐ Eat less
☐ Sleep more
☐ Sleep less
☐ Cry less
☐ Not chew on Big Sib's toys
☐ Other: _____

WE'D DESCRIBE YOU AS

☐ Sleeping beauty
☐ Screaming beauty
☐ A vacuum cleaner
☐ A power pooper
☐ A little cuddle bug
☐ Other: _____

*Like a dream from the heart,
these days will remain fuzzy.*

Parents Tell All

WE'D DESCRIBE OURSELVES AS

- ☐ Sleep-deprived zombies
- ☐ Cave dwellers never leaving the house
- ☐ Camp directors organizing different activities for different age levels
- ☐ Magician's assistants split in two
- ☐ Surfer dudes going with the flow
- ☐ Scientists tracking meals, poops and sleep
- ☐ Miners who struck gold with two wonderful kids

WE'D DESCRIBE BIG SIB AS

- ☐ A love bug always ready with kisses and cuddles
- ☐ A magnet stuck to Mom or Dad
- ☐ A third parent
- ☐ The Tasmanian Devil sweeping through everything in sight
- ☐ A rival vying for toys and attention
- ☐ Baby's best friend
- ☐ A confident young man or young woman
- ☐ Other: _____

Details and thoughts: _____

_____

_____

_____

_____

_____

_____

Big Sib Tells All

THAT'S A BABY?

I THOUGHT I WAS GETTING A

- ☐ Playmate
- ☐ Rival
- ☐ Student to teach
- ☐ Little person to boss around
- ☐ Little me

BUT INSTEAD I'VE GOT

- ☐ A stuffed animal
- ☐ A puppy
- ☐ A dress-up toy
- ☐ Someone to tickle
- ☐ My own baby
- ☐ Something Mom and Dad won't let me play with
- ☐ Other: _____

BEING A BIG SIB WOULD BE A CINCH IF IT WASN'T FOR

- ☐ Sharing toys
- ☐ Sharing Mom
- ☐ Sharing Dad
- ☐ Waiting while Baby _____.
- ☐ Being quiet when Baby naps
- ☐ Other: _____

Details and thoughts: _____
_____
_____
_____

All About Big Sib and Baby

Big Sib is _____ years old.

Big Sib calls Baby_____ .

Things Big Sib loves about Baby: _____
_____
_____

Things Big Sib likes to help with: _____
_____
_____

Things Big Sib can't wait to do with Baby! _____
_____
_____

Funny stories about Big Sib and Baby: _____
_____
_____

EVEN THOUGH YOU'RE LITTLE, I HAVE FUN

☐ Cuddling up with you
☐ Singing songs to you
☐ Reading with you
☐ Caring for you
☐ Other: _____

Use this space for anything!
(Now or Later!)

DRAW A PICTURE, MAKE A HANDPRINT NEXT TO BABY'S,
OR WRITE A LETTER TO BABY WITH MEMORIES
OR THOUGHTS FOR THE FUTURE.

Date: _____

Baby's First Meals

Is Mommy's milk Baby's sole nourishment?
Circle the choices that apply

BABY	**MOM**
Yes, it's yummy	Yes, it's easy
Yes, but I have mixed feelings	Yes, but it's challenging
Almost, but I'm still hungry	I supplement also
No, it's not for me	No, it didn't work out
Other: _____	Other: _____

BABY'S EATING STYLE:

☐ Gorging
☐ Grazing
☐ Graze, nod off, graze, nod off
☐ Finicky—no thanks, maybe later
☐ Speed eating and then spitting up
☐ All of the above—at different times
☐ Other: _____

STRATEGIES FOR KEEPING YOU AWAKE DURING FEEDINGS:

☐ Tickle your feet
☐ Open the windows
☐ Make lots of noise
☐ Baby's always awake during feedings
☐ Peel off your onesies so the cool air will wake you

Favorite spit-up story or details about feeding:

_____
_____
_____
_____

> "So fall asleep love, loved by me."
> ROBERT BROWNING

Baby in Dreamland

WHEN YOU SLEEP, WE WONDER

- ☐ How long it will be before you wake up
- ☐ What you're dreaming about
- ☐ What's behind that beautiful little smile that pops up
- ☐ How you could go from a deep sleep to wide awake and screaming in seconds
- ☐ If we'll ever know that peaceful feeling of sleep again
- ☐ If Big Sib will wake us when we're finally asleep
- ☐ Other: _____

Does Big Sib help with bedtime? _____
_____
_____
_____

Best excuses from Big Sib to avoid bedtime? _____
_____
_____
_____

WHO SLEEPS?

- ☐ Nobody
- ☐ Baby
- ☐ Big Sib
- ☐ Dad
- ☐ Mom
- ☐ It depends on _____

Diaper Drama

Although we've had practice in the diaper department, the challenge comes from

☐ Two kids in diapers
☐ Diapering you and potty training Big Sib
☐ We're out of practice and forgot _____
☐ Remembering to point baby boys down
☐ Having enough diapers and extra clothes for you and Big Sib
☐ Other: _____

Most challenging place to change a diaper: _____
_____

QUICK-THINKING PARENTS

We've used up all the diapers and Baby's dirty again. What do we do? _____
_____
_____
_____

We've got Baby on the changing table when Big Sib
_____
_____

What do we do? _____
_____
_____
_____

"The only thing that is constant is change."

HERACLITIS

Making Change

WHEN BABY GETS A DIAPER CHANGE, BIG SIB

- [ ] Hides in the other room
- [ ] Distracts Baby
- [ ] Helps by handing the diapers and supplies
- [ ] Occasionally changes the diaper!
- [ ] Doesn't care either way
- [ ] Does who knows what?

DADDY DOES DIAPERS?

- [ ] Of course
- [ ] Parents take turns
- [ ] Sometimes
- [ ] Never

Most challenging place to change a diaper: _____

_____

_____

Any funny or frustrating diaper stories? _____

_____

_____

_____

_____

_____

_____

"Even when freshly washed and relieved of all obvious confections, children tend to be sticky."

FRAN LEBOWITZ

Baby's First Baths
SPONGE BATH, BABY TUB & BEYOND!

The best thing about bath time: _____

_____

BATH TIME IS

- ☐ A great time to bond with Baby
- ☐ A fun session with siblings
- ☐ A harrowing experience
- ☐ It depends on the day

Details or descriptions: _____

_____

_____

Baby Bath Happiness Meter

You would rather tear your eyes out.

You scream for a minute then calm down.

You are hesitant but have a good time.

You jump out of our arms to get in.

Challenges, toys, equipment or stories: _____

_____

_____

_____

_____

Family's Post-Baby Hygiene

Parents: Is finding time to shower challenging?

BIG SIB

Bath, shower, deodorant or air freshener? _____

Big Sib's Bath/Shower Happiness Meter

☺	You would rather be vacuumed.
☺☺	You have to be coerced or bribed but do it.
☺☺☹	You love it.
☹☹☹☹	You would spend hours in the shower or bath.

Sibling Stinky Meter

☺	You bathe every day.
☺☺	You bathe every other day.
☺☺☹	You bathe every third day.
☺☹☹☹	You bathe every week.
☹☹☹☹☹	You use a lot of perfume or cologne.

ADD A BATH TIME PHOTO

"Having a two-year-old is kind of like having a blender, but you don't have a top for it."

JERRY SEINFELD

Parenting Two: Survival Skills

SKILLS

- [ ] Swaddling Baby
- [ ] Juggling schedules or needs
- [ ] Selective hearing
- [ ] Patience
- [ ] Optimism
- [ ] Panic
- [ ] Other: _____

HARD OR EASY?

Looking angry when the kids are doing something they shouldn't but are super cute. _____

Things we do to quiet Baby down: _____

TOUGHEST THINGS ABOUT PARENTING TWO

- [ ] Different schedules
- [ ] Different needs
- [ ] Two in diapers
- [ ] Two to feed
- [ ] Finding time for ourselves
- [ ] Other: _____

Details and thoughts: _____
_____
_____

PARENTING AN INFANT AND AN OLDER SIBLING IS

☐ As easy as walking and chewing gum at the same time
☐ As difficult as building a rocket ship to Mars in the bathtub
☐ Somewhere in between.
☐ Other: _____

We are surprisingly good at _____.

RANK THEM FROM BAD TO WORST

☐ Two kids are sick.
☐ Two explosive poops need changing.
☐ Two kids are melting down in public.
☐ Other: _____

RANK THEM FROM GREAT TO SUPER FANTASTIC

☐ Two kids are laughing and playing together.
☐ Two kids are sleeping.
☐ Two kids are cuddling with you.
☐ Other: _____

Details and thoughts: _____

_____
_____
_____
_____
_____
_____
_____
_____
_____
_____

Keep Calm and Carry On

What were some of your earliest worries? _____
_____
_____
_____

Who is the family worrywart? _____
_____
_____
_____

WE WORRY THAT BIG SIB MIGHT

- ☐ Accidentally drop Baby
- ☐ Squeeze Baby too hard
- ☐ Feed Baby marbles, M&Ms, or other chocking hazards
- ☐ Bite or hit Baby
- ☐ Try to return Baby
- ☐ Other: _____

DR. SIB: DID BIG SIB EVER THINK BABY WAS

- ☐ Sick
- ☐ Hungry
- ☐ Bored
- ☐ Not sharing
- ☐ Hogging all the attention
- ☐ Ready to go back where he/she came from
- ☐ Other: _____

Top Three Reasons
WE LOVE BEING YOUR PARENTS

1. _____

2. _____

3. _____

Top Three Reasons
BIG SIB LOVES BEING YOUR BIG SIB

1. _____

2. _____

3. _____

Details and thoughts: _____

_____

_____

_____

_____

_____

65

Baby Olympics

IN MARATHON SLEEPING, YOU WIN

☐ **Gold:** Smashed record by sleeping past 5:00 a.m.

☐ **Silver:** Beat previous _____ hours of sleep
(fill in # of hours)

☐ **Bronze:** Slept in the car seat until we reached the next state

☐ Didn't qualify: _____

IN SPEED SLEEPING, YOU WIN

☐ **Gold:** Head pops up as soon as it goes down

☐ **Silver:** Do 30 seconds even count as a nap?

☐ **Bronze:** Set a personal record with _____ hours straight

☐ Didn't qualify: _____

IN MARATHON NURSING, YOU WIN

☐ **Gold:** Managed to nurse almost nonstop for _____ hours

☐ **Silver:** You didn't stop until Mom pried you off

☐ **Bronze:** Stopped nursing long enough to take a 20-minute nap

☐ Didn't qualify: _____

IN OLYMPIC CRYING, YOU WIN

☐ **Gold:** Your first days you screamed nonstop

☐ **Silver:** Nothing seems to soothe you

☐ **Bronze:** You stopped crying to eat

☐ Didn't qualify: _____

IN POWER POOPING, YOU WIN

- ☐ **Gold:** Changed _____ diapers in one day
- ☐ **Silver:** As soon as your diaper was changed, you soiled the new one
- ☐ **Bronze:** What can we say, your system works
- ☐ Didn't qualify: _____

IN DIARRHEA DIRTY DIAPER DASH, YOU WIN

- ☐ **Gold:** Leaked through diaper and clothes
- ☐ **Silver:** Soiled the new, clean diaper while it was going on
- ☐ **Bronze:** Waited until the new clean diaper was on to poop
- ☐ Didn't qualify: _____

IN LONG-DISTANCE STARVING, YOU WIN

- ☐ **Gold:** Refused to nurse or take a bottle
- ☐ **Silver:** Fell asleep as soon as you latched on
- ☐ **Bronze:** Spit up everything you ate
- ☐ Didn't qualify: _____

ADD A
PHOTO HERE

ADD A
PHOTO HERE

Baby's Firsts/ Family's Firsts

Baby's Firsts/Family's Firsts

Every day is full of firsts. A simple thing like your smile seems magical and makes us feel _____. A laugh, a squeal, even a _____ fills us with joy. It's thrilling to watch you grow and change. Your _____ personality is shining through. It seems like every day you get better at _____. We will never forget the first time you _____. One of your favorite things to do is _____, and you're really attached to _____. Our family is growing and changing with you. Mommy loves (to) _____ with you and Daddy loves (to) _____ with you. Big Sib thinks you're the cutest when you _____ and loves _____ with you. You enjoy repetition and sometimes you want us to _____ nonstop. We are developing routines. Something we do every single day is _____. We _____ these early days of learning and growing with you!

Being Four is so much more!

"Smiling babies should actually be categorized by the pharmaceutical industry as a powerful antidepressant."

JIM GAFFIGAN

Baby's First Smile

THAT SMILE

- [ ] Took us by surprise
- [ ] Swept us off our feet
- [ ] Nearly caused a stampede of cooing grandmas at the market
- [ ] Made us feel even more connected to you
- [ ] Reminds us of one of our favorite people: _____
- [ ] Other: _____

Family Smiles

You make Big Sib smile when _____

_____

_____

_____

_____

_____

_____

You make Mom and Dad smile when _____

_____

_____

_____

_____

_____

_____

> "One joy dispels a hundred cares."
>
> CONFUCIUS

Oh, Happy Days

Some things that make you laugh or smile are:

_____
_____
_____

Your ticklish spots are: _____

The toy that makes you smile most is: _____
_____
_____
_____

Things or activities that make Big Sib smile or laugh:
_____
_____
_____

Things or activities that make Mom smile or laugh:
_____
_____
_____

Things or activities that make Dad smile or laugh:
_____
_____
_____

Big Sib's ticklish spots are: _____

> "There is a world of communication
> which is not dependent on words."

MARY MARTIN

Baby Squawk, Baby Talk

YOU LET US KNOW WHAT YOU WANT BY

- ☐ Screaming
- ☐ Pointing
- ☐ Laughing
- ☐ Crying
- ☐ Throwing a tantrum
- ☐ Babbling
- ☐ Using baby sign language
- ☐ Other: _____

Creative Communication

WE COMMUNICATE WITH YOU BY

- ☐ Smiling
- ☐ Cuddling
- ☐ Talking
- ☐ Baby talk
- ☐ Pointing
- ☐ Sign language
- ☐ Other: _____

Details and thoughts: _____

_____

_____

_____

_____

Baby's First Silly Sounds

YOU'RE

☐ A bubbler
☐ A babbler
☐ A raspberry blower
☐ The strong, silent type
☐ Other: _____

Your first sounds: _____
_____
_____
_____

Describe: _____
_____
_____
_____

Bubble Meter

◯   You never blow bubbles

◯◯   Once in a while a bubble will grow

◯◯◯   Moderately bubbly to loud raspberries

◯◯◯◯   A raspberry smoothie

◯◯◯◯◯   You're a regular bubble machine

SOCIAL BUTTERFLY? TRUE OR FALSE

T/F   You love blowing kisses.
T/F   You love waving bye-bye.
T/F   You sing baby songs.
T/F   You're a natural at patty cake.
T/F   You really don't like to perform.

"Man invented language to satisfy
his deep need to complain."

LILY TOMLIN

Family's First Baby Sounds

SOMETIMES WE'RE SILLY AND COMMUNICATE WITH YOU BY

- [ ] Talking and pointing
- [ ] Blowing bubbles
- [ ] Making raspberries on your belly
- [ ] Tickling you
- [ ] Mimicking your sounds
- [ ] Making sounds for you to mimic
- [ ] Laughing with you
- [ ] Singing to you
- [ ] Other: _____

Which of the above does Baby like the best?

_____

_____

Any special way Baby and Big Sib communicate?

_____

_____

Any songs the family loves to sing? _____

_____

_____

Details and thoughts: _____

_____

_____

_____

Baby's First Real Words

Some of your first words were: _____
_____
_____
_____

The first time you said "dada" we felt: _____
_____
_____

The first time you said "mama" we felt: _____
_____
_____

Your words with lost letters (like "poon" instead of spoon):
_____
_____
_____

Your first and favorite words and expressions:
_____
_____
_____

BABY'S FIRST WORDS FOR

Mom: _____

Dad: _____

Big Sib: _____

Milk: _____

Favorite toy: _____

Pet or Stuffed Animal: _____

Grandma, Grandpa, or other favorite people: _____
_____
_____

"Where is bubu's bopey?"

Family's Baby Words

Do Mom, Dad, or Big Sib have any go-to baby words they use with Baby? If so, what are they? _____

_____

_____

Big Sib's favorite expressions and things to talk about:

_____

_____

_____

Do Mom, Dad, or Big Sib call each other by silly pet names or do baby words ever slip into conversations?

_____

_____

SOMETIMES WHEN WE SPEAK PRIVATELY SO YOU AND BIG SIB WON'T UNDERSTAND WE

- ☐ Use Pig Latin
- ☐ Spell words out
- ☐ Speak (what language) _____
- ☐ Use sign language
- ☐ Wait until we are alone with each other
- ☐ We have nothing to hide ever!
- ☐ Other: _____

Details and thoughts on communicating with Baby:

_____

_____

> *"And we find at the end of a perfect day,
> the soul of a friend we've met."*
>
> CARRIE JACOBS BOND

Baby's First Friends

Your first friends were: _____

_____

_____

_____

_____

This is how you met: _____

_____

_____

_____

_____

_____

Your favorite things to do with friends are: _____

_____

_____

_____

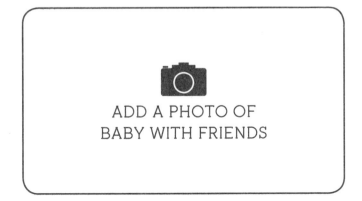

ADD A PHOTO OF
BABY WITH FRIENDS

Baby and Big Sib's Friendship

SIGNS OF A BUDDING FRIENDSHIP
BETWEEN SIBLINGS:

	yes	no	maybe
Cuddling up when reading books	☐	☐	☐
Playing peekaboo	☐	☐	☐
Laughing together	☐	☐	☐
Making jokes only they understand	☐	☐	☐
Wrestling	☐	☐	☐

Playing _____

Other: _____

Details and thoughts: _____

_____

_____

_____

Things Baby and Big Sib like to do together:

_____

_____

_____

_____

BIG SIB SOMETIMES ACTS LIKE BABY'S

☐ Buddy
☐ Protector
☐ Adversary
☐ Boss
☐ Role model
☐ Cheerleader
☐ Partner in crime

> "It is one of the blessings of old friends that you can afford to be stupid with them."

RALPH WALDO EMERSON

Friends like Family

Great memories or funny stories of friends we met through Big Sib: _____

_____

_____

_____

_____

_____

Great memories or funny stories of old friends, family or other important people in our lives: _____

_____

_____

_____

_____

_____

Other best friends: (Can include pets, stuffed animals, and imaginary friends) _____

_____

_____

_____

_____

_____

_____

_____

FIRST SITTERS OR NANNIES

- ☐ We need someone great to take care of you while we're at work.
- ☐ We just need someone to watch you occasionally when we need a night out.
- ☐ We wouldn't leave you with anyone else for now.
- ☐ Big Sib is our built-in babysitter!
- ☐ Other: _____

Our favorite sitter was: _____
because: _____
_____
_____
_____
_____
_____

Details and thoughts: _____
_____
_____
_____
_____
_____
_____

DEAL BREAKERS

- ☐ Texts during interview
- ☐ Chain-smokes
- ☐ Drinks "Diet Coke" out of a paper bag
- ☐ Winks at your partner
- ☐ Other: _____

"Food is an important part of a balanced diet."

FRAN LIEBOWITZ

Baby's First Meals

Any details, thoughts or stories about Baby's liquid diet:

_____

_____

Most challenging place to nurse or feed Baby?

_____

Baby's Nutritional Plate

Baby's First Bottle
(COULD BE BREAST MILK, WATER, OR FORMULA)

Date: _____

GETTING YOU TO TAKE A BOTTLE WAS

☐ Like forcing a vegetarian to eat worms
☐ As easy as giving hugs
☐ You never took a bottle
☐ Other: _____

Family's Meals

THE GO-TO MEAL PLAN WHEN SLEEP DEPRIVED,
TIME STARVED, AND HUNGRY:

- ☐ Toast
- ☐ Pasta
- ☐ Takeout/Order in
- ☐ Cereal—what kind? _____
- ☐ Cooking _____
- ☐ Other: _____

Family's Nutritional Plate

FILL IN THE BLANKS WITH WHAT YOU'RE EATING
BELOW ARE A FEW OPTIONS TO CHOOSE FROM.

Takeout

Leftovers

Cereal

Fluids

Baby food

Whatever we can find in the fridge

Baby's First Solid Food:

When? _____

_____

_____

What? _____

_____

_____

YOU WERE LIKE

- ☐ **Papa Bear:** Feed Me! More! Faster!
- ☐ **Mama Bear:** Okay, I'll give it a try.
- ☐ **Baby Bear:** Yuck! Get that stuff away from me!
- ☐ Other: _____

Details, thoughts, stories, or photo: _____

_____

_____

_____

_____

_____

_____

_____

_____

_____

_____

Watch Us!

BIG SIB'S APPROACH TO EATING:

- ☐ I'd rather not
- ☐ Okay, if I have to
- ☐ I want it all
- ☐ I want mine, yours, and everyone's

BIG SIB'S ROLE AT MEAL TIME:

- ☐ Chef's assistant
- ☐ Menu coordinator
- ☐ Waiter, busboy/girl
- ☐ Diner
- ☐ Food critic
- ☐ Unruly patron

Big Sib's go-to meal & favorite foods: _____

_____

_____

Big Sib hates: _____

_____

_____

Any food allergies or sensitivities?_____

_____

_____

Any baby-friendly restaurants?_____

_____

Baby Whines and Dines

YOU LIKE

☐ Rice Cereal   ☐ Barley Cereal
☐ Oat Cereal   ☐ Applesauce
☐ Bananas   ☐ Avocado
☐ Apricots   ☐ Plums
☐ Pears   ☐ Peas
☐ Sweet Potatoes   ☐ Yellow Squash
☐ Acorn Squash

Anything else? _____

_____

_____

_____

You hate: _____

_____

_____

Any food allergies or sensitivities? _____

_____

_____

BABY'S FAVORITE SEEMINGLY DELICIOUS NON-FOOD ITEMS:

☐ Toys _____
☐ Books _____
☐ Pacifier
☐ Big Sib's shoes
☐ Anything/Everything
☐ Other: _____

> "The secret of success in life is to eat what you like and let the food fight it out inside."

MARK TWAIN

Big Sib/Big Help

WHEN BABY EATS, BIG SIB HELPS BY

- [ ] Demonstrating how to eat
- [ ] Distracting Baby
- [ ] Retrieving food
- [ ] Feeding Baby
- [ ] Hiding or just being busy with something
- [ ] Throwing food (Now who thinks that's helpful?)
- [ ] Other: _____

Any baby foods Big Sib or parents groove on?

_____

_____

_____

Family's Tricks and Treats

Any tricks to get Baby to eat? _____

_____

_____

Any tricks backfire and turn the kitchen into a disaster?

_____

_____

_____

> "I sleep like a baby. I'm up every two hours."
>
> BILLY CRYSTAL

Baby's First Nights

- ☐ You're a good sleeper
- ☐ You fall asleep easily, but you're up in a flash.

You can't get to sleep unless
- ☐ Someone cuddles up with you
- ☐ Someone rocks you
- ☐ Mom nurses you or you've got a bottle
- ☐ Someone sings to you
- ☐ Mom or Dad drives you around the neighborhood
- ☐ Other: _____

Creative or desperate things we do
to get the Baby to go to sleep: _____

_____

_____

Favorite nappy, plush toy, or comfort item: _____

_____

_____

ADD A PHOTO OF
BABY SLEEPING

Parents' Long Nights

Sleep Meter

😴 What is sleep?

😴 😴 Sleep is overrated.

😴 😴 😴 I'll sleep when you go to kindergarten.

😴 😴 😴 😴 Make up for lost sleep with ten-minute naps.

😴 😴 😴 😴 😴 Haven't lost a wink.

IF WE WERE WRITING A BOOK ABOUT LATE-NIGHT HOURS AT OUR HOME, THE TITLE COULD BE

- [ ] *Sleep No More*
- [ ] *Everyone Can Hear You Scream*
- [ ] *I Got Up the Last 9 Times; It's Your Turn*
- [ ] *Zombie Apocalypse*
- [ ] *Pretty Slumbers*
- [ ] *The Never Ending Night*
- [ ] Other: _____

WE LOOK FOR ADVICE IN

- [ ] Every book available
- [ ] The go-to book _____
- [ ] The Internet
- [ ] Friends or relatives
- [ ] We don't need any books or advice
- [ ] Other: _____

Details and thoughts: _____

_____

_____

_____

Baby's Bedtime Rituals

Here's how we do bedtime with Baby: _____

_____

_____

Are Baby and Big Sib like the dynamic duo when getting
ready for bed? Do they brush their teeth and do other
things together or do their own thing? _____

_____

_____

Your favorite part of bedtime is: _____

_____

_____

Our favorite part of bedtime is: _____

_____

_____

Your favorite bedtime stories, books, or lullabies:

_____

_____

_____

BABY THINKS BOOKS ARE

☐ A chew toy
☐ Something nice to bring people together
☐ What's a book?
☐ Other: _____

Family's Bedtime Rituals

Here's how Big Sib does bedtime: _____

_____

_____

Big Sib's favorite part of bedtime is: _____

_____

_____

BIG SIB'S DREAM BEDTIME WOULD INCLUDE:

- ☐ Jumping on the beds
- ☐ Reading books
- ☐ Cuddling up together
- ☐ Taking a bath
- ☐ Something related to electronics (watching TV, gaming, snapchatting, _____)
- ☐ Other:_____

Sleep strategies for Baby: Are Mom and Dad on the same page? _____

_____

_____

	Mom Likes	Dad Likes
Comforting you to help you sleep		
Have Baby self-soothe		
A mixture of both		
Other: _____		

> "Forgive me if I sleep until I wake up."
>
> CHARLES OLSON

WHEN THE KIDS ARE FINALLY ASLEEP, WE

- ☐ Have dinner together and catch up
- ☐ Watch TV
- ☐ Crash
- ☐ Do laundry and other chores
- ☐ Other: _____

THE FIRST TIME YOU SLEPT THROUGH THE NIGHT, WE THOUGHT

- ☐ It was a freak accident
- ☐ It was a miracle
- ☐ We had the wrong baby
- ☐ Time to celebrate! We could finally get back to a normal schedule (yeah, right)
- ☐ Something was wrong with you

WHILE YOU SLEPT THROUGH YOUR FIRST NIGHT, WE

- ☐ Tried to watch TV
- ☐ Lay awake staring at the ceiling
- ☐ Slept peacefully
- ☐ Stayed up waiting for you to wake up
- ☐ Were still up with Big Sib
- ☐ Other: _____

THAT NIGHT, BIG SIB

- ☐ Woke up
- ☐ Kept sleeping
- ☐ Not really sure
- ☐ Other: _____

> "I think I discovered the secret of life—you just hang around until you get used to it."

CHARLES M. SCHULZ

Baby's First Steps Toward Independence

HOLDING HEAD UP
Details: _____

_____

WAVING BYE-BYE / BLOWING KISSES
Details: _____

_____

SITTING UP
Details: _____

_____

ROLLING OVER
Details: _____

_____

CRAWLING
Details: _____

_____

Style: ☐ Traditional ☐ Backward ☐ Belly ☐ Other: _____

CRUISING
Details: _____

_____

_____

_____

Favorite thing to cruise on: _____

*"I learned to walk as a baby,
and I haven't had a lesson since."*

MARILYN MONROE

Baby's First Step

Where was it and who was there to witness it?

_____

_____

IT WAS

- ☐ A lone step and a crash
- ☐ A few steps and a carefully planned fall
- ☐ An awkward dance across the floor
- ☐ A flawless journey from point A to B
- ☐ Spectacular
- ☐ Other: _____

BABY WAS

- ☐ Thrilled
- ☐ Glad when it was over
- ☐ Surprised
- ☐ Uninterested
- ☐ Other: _____

When did Baby really start walking? _____

_____

_____

_____

_____

Family's Stepping-Stones and Milestones

BIG SIB

What's the latest? Any milestones or stepping-stones for Big Sib? _____

_____

_____

_____

_____

_____

_____

_____

PARENTS

What's the latest? Any milestones or stepping-stones for Mom and Dad?_____

_____

_____

_____

_____

> "Asked to switch seats on the plane because I was sitting next to a crying baby. Apparently, that's not allowed if the baby is yours."

ILANA WILES

Baby Tantrum Prevention

Warning signs that you were going to have a tantrum:

_____

_____

You're mostly like to lose it in these situations:

_____

_____

OUR PREVENTION STRATEGIES:

- ☐ Change the subject
- ☐ Pull out a lollipop
- ☐ Jiggle keys or another distraction
- ☐ Sing
- ☐ Resort to electronics
- ☐ Take a drive
- ☐ Other: _____

Things Big Sib does to cheer Baby up: _____

_____

_____

Your name when you're in trouble: _____

_____

> "All of us have moments in our lives that test our courage. Taking our children into a house with a white carpet is one of them."
>
> ERMA BOMBECK

Family Tantrum Prevention

Big Sib sometimes loses their cool when: _____

_____

_____

What pushes Mom's buttons? _____

_____

_____

What pushes Dad's buttons? _____

_____

_____

STRATEGIES WE USE TO KEEP CALM:

- [ ] Count to 10
- [ ] Sing the alphabet
- [ ] Tear out your hair
- [ ] Get angry now, keep calm later
- [ ] Other: _____

THE POWER OF CUTENESS:
Do Big Sib or Baby ever use a smile or an "I love you" to melt away Mom or Dad's meltdown? _____

_____

_____

Baby's First Haircut & Style

When you were _____ old, _____ gave you your first haircut.

YOU

☐ Were scared and cried
☐ Kept trying to grab the scissors
☐ Kept turning to look, which was scary for us
☐ Couldn't care less
☐ Loved the attention
☐ Other: _____

WE FELT

☐ Excited to see your new look
☐ Worried about your curls not growing back
☐ Worried about you getting poked with the scissors
☐ Proud and surprised to see you growing up
☐ Other: _____

You often wear your hair: _____

_____

_____

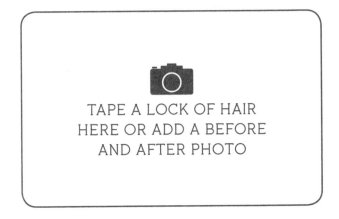

TAPE A LOCK OF HAIR
HERE OR ADD A BEFORE
AND AFTER PHOTO

BABY ROCKS CLOTHES FROM:

- [ ] Big Sib
- [ ] Thrift stores
- [ ] The fanciest catalogues _____
- [ ] The Internet _____
- [ ] Other: _____

Travelling Style

BY CAR:

- [ ] We traded in our _____ for a _____.
- [ ] We expanded when we had Big Sib
- [ ] We are still squished in _____.
- [ ] Who needs a car?
- [ ] Other: _____.

BY FOOT:

- [ ] Single stroller
  - [ ] with skateboard
- [ ] Double stroller
  - [ ] front/back
  - [ ] side to side
- [ ] Baby carrier
- [ ] Baby in carrier & Big Sib in stroller
- [ ] Big Sib walks or _____
- [ ] Other: _____

Details, thoughts including any cool stroller or car accessories: _____

_____

_____

_____

First Attempts at Potty Training

When and what we told you: _____

_____

WERE YOU READY?

☐ Yes
☐ No

Details: _____

_____

_____

BRIBES AND INCENTIVES:

☐ Stickers
☐ M&M's
☐ TV or tablet time
☐ Money or other presents
☐ A family vacation
☐ Special big-kid underwear
☐ For boys, target practice
☐ Other: _____

Did Big Sib help or offer advice? _____

_____

_____

Details, thoughts, and potty stories: _____

_____

_____

"Shut the front door!"

Parents' Potty Mouth

Ever let a curse word slip in the heat
of a parenting moment? _____
_____

Funny story? _____
_____

ACCEPTABLE PG CURSE WORDS MOM, DAD, OR BIG
SIB USE INSTEAD:

- ☐ Oh, poop!
- ☐ Oh, fudge!
- ☐ Oh, tarter sauce!
- ☐ Shiitake mushrooms!
- ☐ Cheese & rice!
- ☐ Shut the front door!
- ☐ Son of a blee-blob!
- ☐ Other: _____

Big Sib's Potty Mouth

Did Big Sib pick up any "bad words" that you hope Baby
won't learn?* _____
_____
_____

*NOTE: THIS IS A FAMILY BOOK, PLEASE ABBREVIATE,
USE CODE, OR CHECK BELOW:

- ☐ *&^%*
- ☐ Bleepin' Bleepin' Bleep

> "Love can change a person the way a parent can change a baby—awkwardly, and often with a great deal of mess."
>
> LEMONY SNICKET

Potty Training Predicaments

MOST CHALLENGING BATHROOM VISITS:

☐ Train station
☐ Superstore
☐ McDonald's or other fast-food restaurant
☐ Porta potty
☐ Other: _____

Did we travel with a potty? _____

Any funny or not so funny potty training stories?

_____

_____

_____

How long did it take to be fully trained? _____

_____

Any tips and tricks that worked especially well?

_____

_____

_____

Somebody Pinch Me!

Use this space for anything!

(MEMORIES, DETAILS, THOUGHTS, PHOTOS,
DRAWINGS, OR EVEN STICKERS.)

ADD A
PHOTO HERE

Favorite Firsts:

Looking back, what were some favorite family firsts?

_____

_____

_____

_____

_____

_____

_____

_____

_____

_____

_____

_____

_____

Now That We're Four

Now That We're Four

Before you arrived you were a mystery, and now you're a treasure! We couldn't imagine life without you. You are so _____ and so full of _____.
There are so many things we like to do together like _____
_____ and
_____. One of your favorite places to go is _____.
You love to _____ and you're a natural at
_____. You and Big Sib love to _____ together.
Now that you're a little older you're starting to enjoy _____
_____. One great memory we have together is _____
_____
_____
_____.
You've changed our lives in such a _____ way.
We're looking forward to a lifetime of memories and adventures together.

We've found happiness galore, now that we're Four.

HABITS WE'VE PICKED UP:

- ☐ We started mixing up the kids names! When rushing to call one, we call the other and then stumble over our tongues.
- ☐ We started singing baby songs out loud at home and under our breath everywhere else we go.
- ☐ Everyone's snacking on teething biscuits, Cheerios, or Goldfish.
- ☐ Multi-multi-multi-tasking.
- ☐ We're always making each other laugh.
- ☐ Other: _____

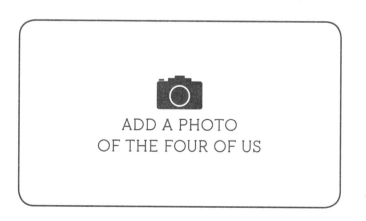

ADD A PHOTO
OF THE FOUR OF US

ADD A PHOTO
OF THE FOUR OF US

Looking Back:
Before We Were Four

BEFORE WE WERE FOUR, YOU WERE A MYSTERY. WE WONDERED

- ☐ What you'd be like
- ☐ How we would juggle everything
- ☐ Who you would look like
- ☐ Other: _____

NOW THAT WE'RE FOUR, WE ARE FILLED WITH GRATITUDE ABOUT

- ☐ The wonderful person you're becoming
- ☐ How much joy you bring to our family
- ☐ How you turn our world upside down. (But in a good way!)
- ☐ Other: _____

BEFORE WE WERE FOUR, WE WORRIED ABOUT

- ☐ Not having enough love for two kids
- ☐ Not having enough time for two kids
- ☐ Not having enough money for two kids
- ☐ Other: _____

BUT NOW THAT WE'RE FOUR, IT'S

- ☐ Like running the love boat—there's an abundance of love for everyone
- ☐ Like running a theater company—there's lots of drama
- ☐ Like running a circus—there's lots of juggling
- ☐ Like a potluck dinner—everyone brings something special to the table.
- ☐ Other: _____

Out and About
(OR OUT AND IN?)

WHICH FAMILY ARE WE?
(IT'S OKAY–SOME FAMILIES CHECK MANY BOXES.)

GETTING OUT OF THE HOUSE:

A. ☐ We get out of the house every chance we get:

    ☐ It's the only way Baby will sleep
    ☐ It's the only way the kids get along
    ☐ We're out a lot, but sometimes lose a kid in the store
    ☐ It's really fun! We love adventures
    ☐ Other: _____

B. ☐ Getting out of the house can be a challenge:

    By the time we get all packed up, one of the kids:
    ☐ falls asleep
    ☐ is starving again
    ☐ needs a diaper changed
    ☐ other: _____

C. ☐ We love staying home and

    ☐ Doing projects (like filling out this memory book!)
    ☐ Cuddling up and reading books
    ☐ Playing _____
    ☐ Other: _____

WHICH FAMILY ARE WE?

AT A RESTAURANT:

- [ ] The family with the perfectly behaved children that everyone fawns over
- [ ] The family that never gets to finish a meal because their kids make a scene
- [ ] The family that clears the restaurant because their screaming kids have chased everyone else away
- [ ] Other: _____

AT THE MOVIES:

- [ ] That magical family that makes it through a movie without disturbing the whole theater
- [ ] The family who walks out of the movie about 20 minutes in because _____
- [ ] The family coming in late because they couldn't get out of the house in time
- [ ] The family whose kids are screaming and throwing popcorn
- [ ] The family that doesn't even try to go to the movies
- [ ] The family who tries to watch a movie at home but falls asleep

"I have found the best way to give advice
to your children is to find out what they want
and then advise them to do it."

HARRY S. TRUMAN

CAREGIVER CONNECTION
(CHECK ALL CHOICES THAT APPLY)

	Mom	Dad	Big Sib
Checks to see if Baby is breathing when asleep	☐	☐	☐
Up in a flash when Baby starts crying	☐	☐	☐
Asks if Baby can be returned	☐	☐	☐
Waits for Baby to self-soothe before getting up	☐	☐	☐
Recognizes Baby's cry in a room full of babies	☐	☐	☐
Gets annoyed at parents for letting their baby cry until realizing it's Baby that's crying.	☐	☐	☐
Makes faces or tickles Baby to cheer Baby up	☐	☐	☐

WITH BABY #1, WE WERE

☐ Nervous wrecks
☐ Sleepwalkers
☐ Blissfully ignorant
☐ Other: _____

NOW WE'RE

☐ Nervous wrecks
☐ Pretty chill
☐ Somewhere in between
☐ Alternating minute by minute
☐ Other: _____

> "When your first baby drops her pacifier, you sterilize it. When your second baby drops her pacifier, you tell the dog: 'Fetch!'"
>
> BRUCE LANSKY

When We Were Three

IF THE BABY'S FOOD DROPPED ON THE FLOOR

- ☐ We'd throw it away
- ☐ We'd throw it away and sterilize the whole kitchen
- ☐ Other: _____

NOW, IF BABY'S FOOD OR PACIFIER FALLS ON THE FLOOR

- ☐ We pick it up and give it to Baby
- ☐ We apply the five-second rule
- ☐ We leave it there until someone gets around to eating it, picking it up, or cleaning it up
- ☐ Baby shares it with the dog depending on who gets to it first
- ☐ We throw it away

LESSONS LEARNED:

- ☐ The five-second rule is now the five-day rule.
- ☐ What doesn't kill you makes you stronger.
- ☐ Germs build immunity.
- ☐ Babies are more resilient than we thought.

Details and thoughts: _____

_____

_____

_____

_____

Sibling Bonding/Sibling Rivalry

AS TIME PASSES, BIG SIB SEES YOU AS

- ☐ A best friend
- ☐ An annoyance
- ☐ A doll to dress
- ☐ A student to teach
- ☐ A competitor
- ☐ Someone to look after and babysit
- ☐ Other: _____

Big Sib started out as our baby,
but now, to you, Big Sib is

- ☐ A rock star
- ☐ A rival
- ☐ A coach
- ☐ A boss
- ☐ A best friend
- ☐ Another parent
- ☐ Other: _____

Details and thoughts: _____

_____

_____

_____

_____

_____

_____

_____

"Two kids are easier than one because they play together. When you've got one, you've got to be the show. When you've got two, you're just an usher."

CHRIS ROCK

Ways Big Sib and Baby are similar: _____
_____
_____
_____
_____

Ways Big Sib and Baby are different: _____
_____
_____
_____
_____

Things Big Sib and Baby like to do together: _____
_____
_____
_____
_____

Fun stories and memories: _____
_____
_____
_____
_____

> "Sometimes being a brother is even better
> than being a superhero!"
>
> MARC BROWN

More about Big Sib & Baby

THINGS BIG SIB TAUGHT BABY:

- [ ] How to make funny faces
- [ ] The ABCs and songs lovely (and occasionally annoying) including _____
- [ ] How to eat vegetables
- [ ] How to brush teeth
- [ ] How to count
- [ ] How to: _____
- [ ] How to: _____

THINGS WE WISH BIG SIB DIDN'T TEACH BABY:

- [ ] Bad words
- [ ] How to climb out of the crib
- [ ] How to sneak into our room
- [ ] How not to eat vegetables
- [ ] How to unfold the laundry
- [ ] How to: _____
- [ ] How to: _____

Details, thoughts, or stories: _____
_____
_____
_____
_____
_____
_____

"In the cookies of life, sisters are the chocolate chips."

THINGS BABY BROUGHT OUT IN BIG SIB:

- ☐ Silliness
- ☐ Competiveness
- ☐ Kindness and nurturing
- ☐ Generosity
- ☐ Protectiveness
- ☐ Anger
- ☐ Patience
- ☐ Other: _____

LETTER OR DRAWING FROM BIG SIB:
(CAN BE DONE AT ANY TIME.)

Date: _____

> "What did my hands do before they held you?"
>
> SYLVIA PLATH

Doubling Up on Love

MOM

I love being a mom of two because: _____

_____

_____

BUT IT'S HARD TO ADJUST TO

- ☐ The lack of downtime
- ☐ Taking orders from 2 bosses
- ☐ Managing the changing schedule
- ☐ Giving kids their fair share of attention
- ☐ Having less one-on-one time with Dad & Big Sib
- ☐ The never ending role of referee
- ☐ Other: _____

DAD

I love being a dad of two because: _____

_____

_____

BUT IT'S HARD TO ADJUST TO

- ☐ The lack of downtime
- ☐ Favoritism
- ☐ Managing the changing schedule
- ☐ The never ending role of referee
- ☐ Having less one-on-one time with Mom & Big Sib
- ☐ The unorganized work environment
- ☐ Other: _____

> "What I do and what I dream include thee."

They Bring Out the Best

 MOM

What I love about Dad that I might not have realized if I didn't have kids: _____

_____

_____

_____

Qualities that make Dad a great dad: _____

_____

_____

 **DAD**

What I love about Mom that I might not have realized if I didn't have kids: _____

_____

_____

_____

Qualities that make Mom a great mom: _____

_____

_____

> "You can only be young once.
> But you can always be immature."
>
> DAVE BARRY

MOM

Original, creative, funny, or kind things Dad does with you that I find adorable: _____

_____

_____

_____

Original, creative, or funny things that
I love to do with you: _____

_____

_____

DAD

Original, creative, funny, or kind things Mom does with you that I find adorable, charming, or sweet: _____

_____

_____

_____

Original, creative, or funny things that
I love to do with you: _____

_____

_____

> "If evolution really works, how come mothers only have two hands?"

MILTON BERLE

Realizations & Parental Super Powers

 **MOM**

WHAT ARE DAD'S PARENTING SUPERPOWERS?

- ☐ Herculean human strength (to carry gear, kids, etc.)
- ☐ Courage to deal with the most difficult situations
- ☐ Super reliability
- ☐ Saint-like patience
- ☐ Bionic ability to bore kids to sleep
- ☐ Extraordinary sense of fun
- ☐ Other: _____

WHAT ARE DAD'S SURVIVAL SUPERPOWERS?

- ☐ Selective hearing
- ☐ Omnipotent optimism
- ☐ Bionic ability to sleep through anything
- ☐ Super sense of humor
- ☐ Endless love
- ☐ Surprising ability to find time for Mom
- ☐ Other: _____

What he could use a little help with: _____

_____

_____

_____

DAD

WHAT ARE MOM'S PARENTING SUPERPOWERS?

- ☐ Herculean human strength (to carry gear, kids, etc.)
- ☐ Baby whisperer: knows just what Baby and Big Sib need
- ☐ Courage to deal with the most difficult situations
- ☐ X-ray vision: able to read to kids with eyes closed
- ☐ Look of steel
- ☐ Super sense of fun
- ☐ Other: _____

WHAT ARE MOM'S SURVIVAL SUPERPOWERS?

- ☐ Selective hearing
- ☐ Superhuman endurance to get through long days
- ☐ Extraordinary ability to love and forgive
- ☐ Never-ending sense of humor
- ☐ Supernatural ability to look good in extreme situations
- ☐ Surprising ability to find time for Dad
- ☐ Other: _____

What she could use a little help with: _____

_____

_____

_____

"We don't even know how strong we are until
we are forced to bring that hidden strength forward."

ISABEL ALLENDE

> "The moments of happiness we enjoy
> take us by surprise. It is not that we seize them,
> but that they seize us."

ASHLEY MONTAGU

Romantic Surprises

Moments we've spent as a family that were surprisingly sweet or romantic: _____

_____

_____

_____

_____

_____

_____

For some, cleaning up spit-up doesn't really qualify as romantic. Record an especially unromantic moment:

_____

_____

_____

_____

_____

_____

_____

_____

"We do not remember days, we remember moments."

CESARE PAVESE

Holding On to Moments

PARENTS

What we want to hold on to about this time in our lives:

_____

_____

_____

_____

Precious moments with Baby we want to remember forever: _____

_____

_____

_____

What we're looking forward to doing with Baby in the future: _____

_____

_____

_____

_____

_____

_____

_____

"A mother discovers with great delight that one does not love one's children just because they are one's children but because of the friendship formed while raising them."

GABRIEL GARCÍA MÁRQUEZ

Falling in Love with You

Here are some of the most adorable things you do that make our hearts burst with love: _____

_____

_____

You are special because: _____

_____

_____

And you're so loveable because: _____

_____

Falling in Love with Family

Four is so much more! Here are some fun things we love doing together: _____

_____

_____

Our family is special because: _____

_____

"Ev'ry morning, ev'ry evening, ain't we got fun."

GUS KAHN & RAYMOND EGAN

Family Fun at Home

We love staying around the house and
doing these things together: _____

_____

_____

Special moments and memories at home: _____

_____

_____

_____

Fun Family Outings

Some fun family outings we've had: _____

_____

_____

_____

_____

Special moments and memories on outings: _____

_____

_____

_____

> "You can discover more about a person in an hour of play than in a year of conversation."
>
> PLATO

Fun One-on-One

Favorite Big Sib-Baby Activities: _____

_____

_____

_____

_____

_____

Favorite Mom-Baby Activities: _____

_____

_____

_____

_____

_____

Favorite Dad-Baby Activities: _____

_____

_____

_____

_____

_____

_____

> "Though we travel the world over to find the beautiful, we must carry it with us, or we find it not."
>
> RALPH WALDO EMERSON

Staycation / Vacation / Day Trip

Describe a wonderful family trip or a vacation the family took together: _____

_____

_____

_____

What made it wonderful? _____

_____

_____

_____

Any challenges or funny stories? _____

_____

_____

_____

ADD A VACATION
PHOTO HERE

> "Who so loves believes the impossible."
>
> ELIZABETH BARRETT BROWNING

Mommy and Daddy Time

Finding time for Mom and Dad to spend together is

- ☐ Impossible
- ☐ Occasional
- ☐ Improbable
- ☐ Sometimes possible between 1 and 1:15 a.m.
- ☐ We set aside _____ for each other
- ☐ Other: _____

What Makes a Date?

DAD

Before we had kids, my idea of a date was: _____

_____

Now, it's: _____

_____

MOM

Before we had kids, my idea of a date was: _____

_____

Now, it's: _____

_____

WHICH COUPLE ARE WE?

- ☐ Date night once a _____ (week, month, decade)
- ☐ We go out for special occasions
- ☐ We never go out
- ☐ We try to eat together when the kids are in bed
- ☐ Lucky if we get to say hi to each other once a day
- ☐ Other: _____

First Home Date
Any Home Date?

WHAT WE DID AND WHAT MADE IT SPECIAL:

- ☐ Made popcorn and started a movie
- ☐ Dressed up and ordered takeout
- ☐ Had a picnic in bed
- ☐ Lit candles
- ☐ Actually had a conversation
- ☐ Read books, watched TV, or just chilled
- ☐ Other: _____

Was it planned or spontaneous? _____

_____

_____

When we have time alone together in the evening,
we usually _____

_____

_____

_____

CHALLENGE: HOW LONG CAN WE LAST WITHOUT TALKING
ABOUT THE KIDS?

Romance Reinvented

DATE NIGHT REDEFINED: WHAT QUALIFIES FOR A DATE?

MOVIE?

- ☐ Going out to the movies–just the parents!
- ☐ Going out to the movies with kids
- ☐ Cuddling up together when kids are asleep
- ☐ Putting on an animated film and ignoring the kids
- ☐ Watching a movie with the kids all over us
- ☐ Forget the movie
- ☐ Other: _____

DINNER?

- ☐ For two, out of the house
- ☐ For two, at home (Sometimes one watches the other eat because it's late.)
- ☐ For four, it's more a family date
- ☐ For four, with each kid entertained with electronics, a book, toys, or someone napping
- ☐ At a play-space/restaurant where kids can play and parents may get to talk
- ☐ Other: _____

Details, thoughts, memories or funny stories: _____

_____

_____

_____

_____

_____

_____

FIRST LEAVE-THE-HOME DATE

WOW! Finally!
Approximate date, year or decade: _____

What we did: _____
_____
_____
_____
_____

How we felt: _____
_____
_____
_____

WHO WANTED TO

	Mom	Dad
Call home immediately	☐	☐
Make a break for the border	☐	☐
Rush back to check on the baby	☐	☐
Stay close by just in case	☐	☐
Come home and be a fly on the wall	☐	☐
Have a great time and enjoy the evening	☐	☐
Plan another date immediately!	☐	☐
Other: _____	☐	☐

IS BIG SIB OLD ENOUGH TO BABYSIT?

☐ Yes
☐ No way
☐ Other: _____

We're More than Four!

FRIENDS & FAMILY

These loved ones really spoil you: _____

_____

_____

Here's some fond memories, funny stories or activities you enjoy doing with grandparents, cousins, aunts or other loved ones: _____

_____

_____

_____

_____

_____

_____

_____

Here's some fond memories, funny stories or activities you enjoy doing with friends: _____

_____

_____

_____

_____

_____

_____

Major Dates
and I Can't Waits

First holidays, birthdays, and more

Major Dates and I Can't Waits

You're growing up before our eyes. How did you get so _____

_____? It's amazing

and wonderful to watch you change. When you were a newborn,

you couldn't even _____, and now you're _____

_____. When you were

little, you really loved (or loved to) _____

_____. Your first birthday was _____

_____.

Everyone is so delighted with all your new tricks and talents

including _____ and _____

_____, and how everyday you're more and

more _____.

Holidays are _____ with

you. Our favorites are _____ and

_____ because _____

_____.

A great holiday food we enjoy on _____

is_____. If we had one special thing

to tell you as you're growing up it would be _____

_____

_____. We also want to tell you how proud

and happy we are that you're ours.

We adore being Four!

Baby's First Celebrations

Any formal party, ceremony or celebration to welcome Baby into the world? _____

_____

_____

What was it? _____

Where was it held? _____

Who came? _____

_____

_____

Did Baby even notice? _____

Any fun gifts? _____

_____

_____

ADD A PHOTO

> "Cheers to a new year and another chance
> for us to get it right."
>
> OPRAH WINFREY

We're having a party!

Baby's first holidays: _____

_____

_____

_____

Christmas, Hanukkah, or other winter celebration

Some holiday fun or traditions: _____

_____

_____

What was Baby's favorite part?_____

_____

_____

Details and thoughts:_____

_____

_____

_____

_____

New Year's Eve or New Year's Day

TOP FAMILY RESOLUTIONS

Any New Year's fun or traditions? _____

_____

_____

Did anyone stay up until midnight? _____

IDEA: WHY WAIT UNTIL MIDNIGHT TO CELEBRATE? BRING IN THE
NEW YEAR AT 7:00 P.M. WITH A COUNTDOWN AND NOISEMAKERS!

Halloween

Costumes! (Matching / Mismatching / Family Theme?):

_____

_____

Any Halloween fun or traditions? _____

_____

_____

What happened to the candy? _____

_____

Mother's Day!

MOTHER'S DAY FANTASY:

- ☐ Sleeping late
- ☐ Breakfast in bed
- ☐ Other: _____

REALITY CHECK:

This is what really happened: _____

_____

_____

Any Mother's Day traditions? _____

_____

_____

Father's Day!

DADDY'S DAY FANTASY:

- ☐ Sleeping late
- ☐ Breakfast in bed
- ☐ Other: _____

REALITY CHECK:

This is what really happened: _____

_____

_____

Any Father's Day traditions? _____

_____

Favorite Holidays & Family Gatherings

Memories, thoughts, or photos from favorite holidays or family gatherings:

Baby at One

Stats (height, weight, or level of cuteness): _____

_____

_____

Baby's personality: _____

_____

_____

_____

Baby loves: _____

_____

_____

_____

Baby hates: _____

_____

_____

_____

Achievements or talents: _____

_____

_____

_____

Unforgettable moment(s): _____

_____

_____

_____

"I wish there was a way to know you're in the good old days before you've actually left them."

"ANDY BERNARD," THE OFFICE

Family When Baby Is One

Big Sib's age and interests: _____
_____
_____

How has Big Sib changed since Baby came along?
_____
_____

What about having a younger sibling
surprises Big Sib the most? _____
_____

 PARENTS

Here's some ways we've changed since Baby arrived:
_____
_____

Here's some things about being parents of two
that surprise us most: _____
_____
_____

> "Where there is love there is life."
>
> MAHATMA GANDHI

Baby Loves

Music: _____
_____
_____

Books: _____
_____
_____

Food: _____
_____
_____

People—real, imaginary, or on TV: _____
_____
_____

Animals—plush, breathing, or on TV: _____
_____
_____

Activities: _____
_____
_____

We can't stop bragging about how Baby: _____

_____

_____

_____

_____

_____

_____

⏱ TIME CAPSULE

If Baby could put all his or her favorite things in a time capsule, what would he or she pack? _____

_____

_____

_____

_____

_____

⏱ TIME CAPSULE

If we could pack some of our favorite things in a time capsule, what would we pack? _____

_____

_____

_____

_____

Baby's First Birthday

What did we do? _____
_____
_____

Who came? _____
_____
_____
_____
_____

Triumph or disaster? _____
_____
_____

Feelings: _____
_____
_____
_____

ADD A PHOTO OF
BABY AT ONE

> "We all have our time machines. Some take us back, they're called memories. Some take us forward, they're called dreams."
>
> JEREMY IRONS

A Letter to Baby at One

Date: _____

Dear_____,

_____

_____

_____

_____

_____

_____

_____

_____

_____

_____

_____

_____

_____

_____

_____

_____

_____

_____

Baby at Two

Stats (height, weight, or level of cuteness): _____

_____

_____

Baby's personality: _____

_____

_____

_____

Baby loves: _____

_____

_____

_____

Baby hates: _____

_____

_____

_____

Achievements or talents: _____

_____

_____

_____

Unforgettable moment(s): _____

_____

_____

_____

Family, Too.

BIG SIB

Big Sib's age and interests: _____

_____

How has Big Sib changed since Baby came along?

_____

_____

What does Big Sib love about being a big sib?

_____

_____

Any milestones or stepping-stones for Big Sib?

_____

PARENTS

What do you love about being parents of two kids?

_____

_____

What's new now that Baby's two? _____

_____

_____

Any milestones or stepping-stones for Mom and Dad?

_____

Baby Loves

Music: _____

Books: _____

Food: _____

People—real, imaginary, or on TV: _____

Animals—plush, breathing, or on TV: _____

Activities: _____

We can't stop bragging about how you: _____

_____

_____

_____

_____

⏱ TIME CAPSULE

If we could pack some of our favorite things in a time capsule, what would we pack? _____

_____

_____

_____

_____

> "I look to the future because that's where
> I'm going to spend the rest of my life."

GEORGE BURNS

Two, Plus—I Can't Wait

BIG SIB

MOMENTS I LOOK FORWARD TO:

1. _____
2. _____
3. _____

MOM

MOMENTS I LOOK FORWARD TO:

1. _____
2. _____
3. _____

Thoughts and feelings: _____

_____

DAD

MOMENTS I LOOK FORWARD TO:

1. _____
2. _____
3. _____

Thoughts and feelings: _____

_____

Closing Note to Baby

Date: _____

Dear _____ ,

_____

_____

_____

_____

_____

_____

_____

_____

_____

_____

_____

_____

_____

_____

_____

_____

_____

_____

_____

_____

_____

_____

"The stories we love best do live in us forever."

J. K. ROWLING

Memories and Milestones

SO MANY FUN, PRECIOUS MEMORIES, AND SO MANY MORE ON THE WAY. USE THIS SPACE TO LOOK BACK OR LOOK FORWARD.

USE THESE PAGES FOR MORE PHOTOS, LETTERS, AND MEMORIES.

Acknowledgments

I'm happy to have this opportunity to thank some of the family, friends, and associates who offered their time, support and smarts to help me with this book.

For starters, my husband and partner, Allan Molho; my children, Willa and Nicky; my mom, Myrna G. Weiner (read: *Magical Genie*), and dad, Sy Weiner, and Allan's parents, Rudy and Roz Molho, as well as my writers group, especially the anchors of the group, Sonia Jaffe Robbins and Maureen Hossbacher, and these great friends doubling as arm-chair editors and focus groups: Rochelle Klempner, Rachel Meyers, Carolyn Turvey, Fabienne Peyrat, Robin Halloran, Jessica Weigmann, Stacie Evans, and Tamara Fish. Thank you, thank you, thank you.

And thank you to my publisher, Cedar Fort, Inc, Bryce Mortimer and the entire crew of editors and designers who cared so much and worked so hard to bring this book and *When We Became Three* to life and who continue to shepherd them into the world. Finally, thank you Marc J. Block and, from the Authors Guild, Michael Gross and Umair Kazi for your time and professional advice.

About the Author

Jill Caryl Weiner is a journalist and the author of the best-selling memory book for first-time parents *When We Became Three: A Memory Book for the Modern Family*. She's written on a broad range of parenting and education-related subjects from homeschooling and kids playing chess for *The New York Times* and *The Wall Street Journal* to innovative educational apps and decorating a pregnant belly for *Time Out New York Kids* and *Mom365*. She's also written essays and articles on other topics including sports and New York City for a variety of publications and websites.

Jill's brothers used to joke about how they cried when she was born. While the joke could be funny at a party, Jill wanted a smoother, more welcoming transition for her son. She wanted her daughter, her first-born, to understand that sharing the spotlight with an adorable co-star wouldn't make her less of a superstar in her parents' eyes, and that being a Big Sib could be an important position and a lot of fun! Keeping sibling and family dynamics in mind, Jill has created *When We Became Four*, the meaningful, fun and flexible memory book that fosters communication, sparks the imagination and can be enjoyed by the whole expanding family.

She lives in New York City with her husband and two children.

To learn more about Jill and her writing, visit her website: www.jillcarylweiner.com